My Final Work of
Divine Indifference

Avatar Adi Da Samraj
Adi Da Samrajashram, 2007

My Final Work of Divine Indifference

Wherein I Constantly Abide Only <u>As</u> I <u>Am</u>,
In Divine and Avatarically Responsive
Transcendental Spiritual Regard of all-and-All

BY THE AVATARIC GREAT SAGE,

Adi Da Samraj

THE DAWN HORSE PRESS
MIDDLETOWN, CALIFORNIA

NOTE TO THE READER

All who study the Way of Adidam or take up its practice should remember that they are responding to a Call to become responsible for themselves. They should understand that they, not Avatar Adi Da Samraj or others, are responsible for any decision they make or action they take in the course of their lives of study or practice.

The devotional, Spiritual, functional, practical, relational, and cultural practices and disciplines referred to in this booklet are appropriate and natural practices that are voluntarily and progressively adopted by members of the practicing congregations of Adidam (as appropriate to the personal circumstance of each individual). Although anyone may find these practices useful and beneficial, they are not presented as advice or recommendations to the general reader or to anyone who is not a member of one of the practicing congregations of Adidam. And nothing in this book is intended as a diagnosis, prescription, or recommended treatment or cure for any specific "problem", whether medical, emotional, psychological, social, or Spiritual. One should apply a particular program of treatment, prevention, cure, or general health only in consultation with a licensed physician or other qualified professional.

My Final Work of Divine Indifference is formally authorized for publication by the Free Sannyasin Order of Adidam. (The Free Sannyasin Order of Adidam is the senior Cultural Authority within the formal gathering of formally acknowledged devotees of the Avataric Great Sage, Adi Da Samraj.)

Produced by the Dawn Horse Press,
a division of the Avataric Pan-Communion of Adidam.

International Standard Book Number: 978-1-57097-234-8

CONTENTS

INTRODUCTION

7

I Am Perfectly Beyond The East
and Perfectly Free In The West

11

Indivisible Perfect Space:
Neither Outer Nor Inner
<u>Is</u> The Space of Reality Itself

23

Walk-About To Me:
My Self-Submission-Time
Has Come To An End

49

My Final Work Is <u>Me</u>—Alone

61

INTRODUCTION

Through a process of supreme Mystery, ultimate Paradox, and unimaginable Grace, Reality Itself has Avatarically Appeared here in bodily (human) Form—as the Avataric Great Sage, Adi Da Samraj.

Through His Avataric Birth and Work here, Avatar Adi Da Is the Conjoining of Reality Itself with the entirety of the cosmic domain. That unspeakably auspicious Conjoining required Avatar Adi Da to undergo an unprecedented Ordeal of "Learning" what "ego" is and Demonstrating the full process of going beyond every vestige of egoity.

Following that period of "Learning" and Demonstration (which lasted until 1970, when He was thirty years of age), Avatar Adi Da entered into a great period of Teaching and Revelation. Just as His time of "Learning" and Demonstration had required His Self-Submission to humankind, His time of Teaching and Revelation continued to require such Self-Submission—so that He could effectively relate to and Instruct ordinary human beings, in their lack of preparedness for the real Transcendental Spiritual process.

The story of this great Work of "Learning", Demonstration, Teaching, and Revelation is summarized in *The Avatar of What Is: The Divine Life and Work of Adi Da*, by Carolyn Lee, and is told in great detail by Adi Da Himself in His Spiritual Autobiography, *The Knee Of Listening*.

Just as Avatar Adi Da was required to "Learn" the life of human limitation, He also had to undergo an immense process of "Shedding" His voluntary Self-Submission and Re-"Emerging", in His bodily (human) Form, as purely Himself—the Divine Avataric Incarnation of Conscious Light.

That dual process—of "Learning" and then "Shedding"—has now reached a point of full Completion. Such is the extraordinary Communication Avatar Adi Da makes in *My Final Work of Divine Indifference.* Now the Divine Avataric Incarnation of Conscious Light Abides Free of any necessity to Teach—and, thus, Free to Retire into His Divine Indifference. That Retirement signifies not an "end" to His Divine Avataric Work, but (rather) His Freedom to be entirely concentrated in His Most Profound Work—of forever Blessing all beings and things.

The essays in this book are taken from one of Avatar Adi Da's primary Revelation-Texts, *The Aletheon: The Practice and The Realization of The Divine Acausal Reality-Principle.* "Aletheon" is a word coined by Adi Da Samraj, based on the Greek word "aletheia", meaning "Truth". Pronounced "ah-LAY-thee-yon" (and, thus, evoking sacred spaces such as the "Pantheon" or the "Parthenon"), the name of this text means "That Which Is (or Contains) the Truth".

I Am Perfectly Beyond The East and Perfectly Free In The West

I.

My Appearance in this "world" is a Divine Avataric Intervention. The Purpose of My bodily (human) Appearance here is the Divine Liberation of all of humankind—not merely the human beings of the East or the human beings of the West, but all human beings (and, indeed, all beings and things altogether).

Having (of historical necessity) been Born in the West, and because of the Ultimacy of My Divine Avataric Purpose here, I have had to Suffer the now-universal "Westernizing" of existence. I was brought up in a circumstance that, outwardly, did not have anything to do with esotericism—yet, from Birth, I was Fully Awake, and Utterly Coincident with the Fullness of Transcendental Spiritual Divine Self-Realization.

My Birth in the West required Me to Undergo a tremendous Ordeal, so that I would be fully Equipped to Address everyone—not only relative to the Great Matter of Divine Self-Realization, but also relative to the characteristic limitations that constitute the universal bondage of humankind in this "late-time" (or "dark" epoch). Fundamental to that bondage is the "Westernization" of the ego.

Much of the Process of My Divine Avataric Lifetime here has been one of (first) "Learning" the Westerner's bondage, and (then) Shedding My Submission to that grossly-bound orientation. Such is the Divine Avataric Self-Submission Whereby I Manifested My Absolute Commitment to Serve everyone. In the Years of My Divine Avataric Self-Submission to "Westernized" humankind, I Did everything That I could possibly Do for the sake of the "late-time" all-and-All. Now I must not (and cannot) continue to be Thus Submitted.

The only-by-Me Revealed and Given Way of Adidam is not a "Western" Way.

The only-by-Me Revealed and Given Way of Adidam is the Way for the totality of humankind.

The only-by-Me Revealed and Given Way of Adidam is not characterized by the limitations of either the West or the East (or the limitations of either the Omega disposition or the Alpha disposition). The only-by-Me Revealed and Given Way of Adidam is entirely and only about the Divine Truth of Reality Itself—without cultural prejudices of any kind.

The only-by-Me Revealed and Given Way of Adidam is, from the beginning, established in the Always Prior Context That Is the Intrinsically egoless and Indivisible Divine Self-Nature, Self-Condition, and Self-State of Reality Itself.

Thus, the only-by-Me Revealed and Given Way of Adidam does not begin with the "Westernized" disposition to seek for fulfillment of the egoic and psycho-physically defined separate "self", nor does It begin with the Easternized disposition to seek for escape from the egoic and psycho-physically defined separate "self".

Most Perfect Divine Self-Realization Is Reality Itself.

Reality Itself Is the Always Prior Self-Condition of all-and-All.

Reality Itself Is the Root and Basis of the Way of Adidam.

Reality Itself Is Indivisibly Self-Manifested and Self-Revealed—not by including both East and West, but by "Radically" (or Always Priorly "At-the-Root") Transcending both East and West.

Reality Itself Is Beyond Alpha and Omega.

I have unreservedly Endured This Ordeal of Divine Avataric Self-Submission to, and subsequent Shedding of My Self-Submission to, the Western adaptation. I have Voluntarily Suffered that adaptation, and I have entirely Understood it. I have Instructed everyone relative to the "radical" transcending of the grossly-bound Western adaptation, and also relative to all the responsibilities that must be exercised in the gross physical domain. Now, there is no "equipment" remaining in This Body to endure any further Self-Submission to the gross orientation of the West.

The Way of Adidam is not about out-growing the Western (or Omega) disposition and then taking up the Eastern (or Alpha) disposition and growing in that until you attain Realization. No.

Altogether, the Realization of Reality Itself is not something one can "grow toward".

The only-by-Me Revealed and Given Way of Adidam begins with Me—with My Perfectly egoless Divine Avataric Person and My Inherently egoless Divine Avataric Self-Nature, Self-Condition, and Self-State, Which Is the Inherently and Perfectly egoless Divine Transcendental Spiritual Self-Nature, Self-Condition, and Self-State of Reality Itself.

The only-by-Me Revealed and Given Way of Adidam begins with Me—always now, always today.

The only-by-Me Revealed and Given Way of Adidam begins with tacit participation in My Divine State of Self-Realization.

The only-by-Me Revealed and Given Way of Adidam is about heart-recognizing Me, being moved to Me, accepting My discipline, and practicing in the profoundest terms.

It has been required of Me to Suffer profoundly the Ordeal of being Born into the Omega circumstance, Adapting to it, "Learning" all of its limitations, fully Understanding it—and, then, being entirely Purified of it and Making My Teaching-Communication about it. In the midst of that immense Process, I Suffered Yogic death several times—to the point where I have now Shed all Western associations.

Coincidently, I have Endured the same Process of "Learning" and Shedding in relation to the Eastern (or Alpha) dimension of human existence. I thoroughly "Learned" everything about the processes of the fourth, the fifth, and the sixth stages of life—in infinite detail. I have Suffered all of that, Understood it, Transcended it, and Taught about it. In that Process of "Learning" the Alpha disposition, I have Undergone many Yogic deaths—ultimately, Passing entirely Beyond the Alpha disposition and Shedding all of it.

Now, all is Shed. I have none of that left anymore—East or West, Alpha or Omega.

The Way of Adidam does not begin from a point of limitation, which you must then grow beyond. The Way of Adidam begins with Me. The Way of Adidam is the Way of the relationship to Me—Always Already Prior to and Beyond all limitations.

You must not reduce the Way I have Revealed and Given to something that accommodates you in your ego-patterning. Because I was Born in the West and largely Taught in the West, My devotees tend to "revise" Adidam in the Western (or Omega) manner. However, "revised" Adidam is not the Way I have Revealed and Given. The Way I have Revealed and Given is simply My Person. That Is "It". That Is the Way of Adidam.

The Way of Adidam is not any manner of living based on your egoically separate "self"—and, thus and thereby, based on the accumulated psycho-physical patterning (or conditioning) to which you are already adapted and to which you are bound, and in which you are, by tendency, persisting. I have Revealed and Given a Way in Which you turn out of all of that, by always turning to Me—whether you are born in the West or born in the East. If you rightly and truly practice the Way of Adidam, you are constantly (moment to moment) whole bodily turned to Me—with all four of the psycho-physical faculties always turned out from the patterning to which you are bound, and (thus and thereby) turned into heart-Communion with Me.

When you are thus whole bodily turned to Me, you are inevitably moved to accept all of the by-Me-Given responsibilities for right life. By all these by-Me-Given devotional and right-life Means, you are entered into My House, the Domain of Transcendental Spiritual Communion with Me, and you grow in That.

As long as you are working on yourself, you are still trapped in the context of the first six stages of life—and, in

16

most cases, in the context of the first three stages of life (or the life of mere gross functionalism and grossly-adapted seeking). Real Spiritual life is "from the top down", not "from the ground up". Therefore, the Way I have Revealed and Given does not begin from the "platform" of the first three stages of life. The Way I have Revealed and Given begins with <u>Me</u>. The Way of Adidam is <u>only</u> heart-recognition of Me and heart-response to Me—turning to Me, following My Instructions, conforming to Me, serving Me, and entering into moment to moment heart-Communion with Me. The Way of Adidam is <u>only</u> that—not any kind of Western "program" or Eastern "program".

I am not Western—and I am not Eastern. I Am the Divine Avataric Presence here, the Divine Avataric Intervention here—neither of the East nor of the West, neither Alpha nor Omega.

I Am That Which Is Prior to <u>all</u> of this Alpha-Omega "world".

II.

I have Revealed and Given a Way that <u>every</u> human being can practice.

I Made My Divine Avataric Self-Submission and (on That Basis) Did My Divine Avataric Teaching-Work and My Divine Avataric Revelation-Work—and now I am Finished with All of That.

Now I am Retired into the Divine Self-Domain of My Own Person.

Now, and forever hereafter, I Am Only and Effortlessly Divinely Avatarically Self-"Emerging", here and everywhere in the cosmic domain.

Therefore, everyone should now (and forever hereafter) come to Me on That Basis.

I Am Beyond (and altogether Prior to) the Alpha domain of the East. And I can no longer Extend Myself into the Omega domain of the West.

Individuals should approach Me fully prepared—by having already and fully studied the Teaching-Revelation I have Given, and by having already and fully adapted the totality of their lives to the necessary Lawfulness of right relationship to Me, as I have clearly Described it.

Individuals should come to Me because they recognize Me at heart, and accept Me at heart as the Divine Heart-Master—such that they are truly Mastered by Me, and are (Thus and Thereby) able to really participate in My Divine Avataric Self-Transmission of My Transcendental Spiritual Divine Self-Nature, Self-Condition, and Self-State.

I no longer have the capability to associate with people in any conventional manner whatsoever. This is not merely a matter of My Disposition. The mechanism to do so literally no longer exists in Me. In the Great Events of Yogic Death Which I have Undergone, there was the actual Disintegration of the various levels of patterning that I Carried, by virtue of the Born Vehicle of Franklin Jones and the Deeper-Personality Vehicle of Ramakrishna-Vivekananda (and all the "Causative" Births that Preceded Them). In each Great Event of Yogic Death, an aspect of that patterning fell away—because I had Sufficiently Done the Work I was Born to Do with that aspect of the "Equipment" of This Divine Avataric Body-Mind.

I Am on Fire. I cannot suppress My State any more. I am Finished with all of "it"—all of "it"! This Is the Extreme of My Divine Avataric Self-"Emergence"-Time.

In the Years of My Divine Avataric Teaching-Work and Divine Avataric Revelation-Work, I Submitted Myself to people just as they are—worldly people, public people, ordinary people. Through that Great Process of Divine Avataric Self-Submission, I "Learned", Noticed, Dealt With, and Understood everyone and everything—and I Addressed everyone and everything with My Divine Avataric Word of Instruction.

Right relationship to Me is not a matter of being "comfortable" with Me. I am not here to be your social relation. I Am Just As I Am.

My egoless Divine Transcendental Spiritual Self-State <u>Is</u> "Who" I <u>Am</u>—and to "Whom" you must come. My Action Masters people—and Blesses them with My Divine Avataric Transcendental Spiritual Self-Transmission. Such Blessing Is What I Am here to Do.

III.

I also Teach the walls, the trees, the dogs. It is not that I Give a verbal Teaching to them. My Communication to them is non-verbal.

Because It <u>Is</u> Reality Itself, My Divine Avataric Teaching-Revelation and My Divine Avataric Transcendental Spiritual Self-Transmission are usable and Realizable by all beings, and even by every "thing"—including something as apparently inert as a wall, or a room, or a building.

<u>All</u> of conditionally manifested existence can be Divinely Transcendentally Spiritually Awakened and made right by Me. <u>All</u> of conditionally manifested existence can be turned to Me. There is not anything—no "one", no entity, no form, no sign, no process, no event, no happening, no appearance—that cannot be devoted to Me, turned to Me, and combined with Me in the egoless Divine Transcendental Spiritual Manner. Everyone and everything can be turned to Me. The entire "world" can be turned to Me. The cosmic domain can—and should—be entirely and Perfectly turned to Me. I Am the Divine Avataric Person and Self-Revelation of Reality Itself.

Human beings tend to make overly much of My Teaching-Revelation as a verbal matter—as something with which to entertain their minds. My Teaching-Revelation is actually a <u>process</u>, not merely a verbal Communication. My Teaching-Revelation Is the process of "radical" devotion and right life That <u>Is</u> "Perfect Knowledge"—because that entire process is in heart-Communion with Me, transcending (and Free-Standing, Always Prior to) the "point of view" (or conditionally and psycho-physically "located") position.

The dog in My House can do it. So can you. My verbal Address is certainly usable to human beings. Because human beings exercise the verbal mind, the verbal mind must be Addressed by Me. However, if you merely "think about" My verbal Address, you are wasting your life in the "talking school".

The Process of Divine Avataric Self-Realization is of a Perfectly (or Always Priorly) egoless Transcendental Spiritual Nature. If you understand what the Way of Adidam is about, then you will apply yourself and adapt quickly, and look to mature in the process readily. There are real requirements, to be sure, and they are not to be compromised—but they can be fulfilled by <u>anyone</u>.

Indivisible
Perfect Space

Neither Outer Nor Inner
Is The Space of Reality Itself

I.

I Speak in reference to the limitations in Westerners (or Occidentals) and the limitations in Easterners (or Orientals)—but I (Myself) am <u>not</u> to be equated with either the Western or the Eastern limits, or characteristics of orientation and understanding.

By patterned tendency, people (in accordance with the conventions of their tradition of adaptation) listen out of one ear or the other, but not with both. That is to say, it is as if Easterners listen with one ear (or on one side of the brain) and Westerners with the other. The whole of humanity is, in that sense, schizophrenic, having divided itself into two separate spheres—as if the two halves of the brain were disconnected from each other.

My Revelation is of My Own egoless Transcendental Spiritual Self-Nature, Self-Condition, and Self-State—Self-Revealing Reality Itself, as a Whole, as a Totality, and (Thus) <u>As</u> Prior Indivisibility, Self-Unity, and Singleness. Therefore, to rightly recognize Me is to tacitly heart-recognize Me <u>As</u> That.

I Demonstrate Totality to here. I Reveal Reality Itself, Which <u>Is</u> Divine in Its Totality—not fractioned by humankind, not changed or limited by humankind.

I Function in an egoless Transcendental Spiritual (and, Thus, Super-normal) Manner. I am not here limited as a gross (physical) phenomenon.

When I am Really "Located", My Transcendental Spiritual Self-Transmission is literal and undeniable. My Transcendental Spiritual Self-Transmission Is the "Proof" that Reality—and the "world" altogether—is of an entirely different Nature than people otherwise suppose.

When people "Locate" and "Know" Me in that Real manner, they no longer continue in the merely-gross pattern of egoic "worldliness". To "Locate" and "Know" Me, Transcendentally and Spiritually, is Inherently Transformative. If you

"Know" Me Transcendentally and Spiritually, you are transformed. If you are not transformed, then you do not "Know" Me Transcendentally and Spiritually.

What I am Self-Manifesting here—including My Teaching altogether—Exceeds the limitations of traditional Eastern culture, just as It Exceeds the limitations of traditional Western culture.

Therefore, I must be heart-recognized and "Known" As I Am—Beyond, and Prior to, both Alpha (or the Eastern mode of "knowing") and Omega (or the Western mode of "knowing").

My Consciousness is not Itself local (or localized), and not bound by "point of view". Because I am of a Transcendental Spiritual Nature, My Sensitivity is Universalized. Therefore, I am Self-Extended to (literally) everywhere and everyone.

From Birth, I have been an egoless Non-local "Personality"—always having to Suffer and Address people who are limited to "point of view" in the body.

Human beings are ego-bound to "point of view"—locked into a physical shape, a conditionally apparent and limited "self"-image. In any case, Reality Itself is not a "point of view". Therefore, Divine Self-Realization—or Most Perfect Realization of the Self-Nature, Self-Condition, and Self-State of Reality Itself—is Non-local, and (therefore) Most Perfect Reality-Realization Outshines the body-mind and the "world". That Is True. That Is the Truth.

That is why renunciation and Realization are the same. It is not that there is something about the body that is to be avoided—as if it were a kind of trap, in and of itself. It is simply that Most Perfect Realization of Reality Itself is Inherently egoless—and, therefore, Intrinsically (and literally) Non-local.

My devotees must never relate to Me as a merely localized entity. My devotees must always relate to Me As I Am.

26

If you heart-recognize Me, then you "Know" this. I am not confined by the Body. I am (while I live) merely in <u>apparent</u> association with the Body—for the Sake of beings. That is all. I am not of a local nature. There is no ego "inside" This Body. If you "pin" Me in the Body—seeing Me only in terms of the gross body and the social personality—then you are not aware of Me.

Through the bodily eyes, I can look into the room, but I am literally seeing everywhere. It is an extraordinary Process, Beyond ordinary human comprehension—but It is Really So.

I am Associated with <u>all</u> the dimensions of Reality—altogether and everywhere.

I am not localized in a body or in a mind. I have an apparent association with This Body, for the Sake of everyone—but It is <u>I</u> (<u>As</u> I <u>Am</u>) Who am Associated with This Body.

I am not an egoic entity. Therefore, I am not aware in egoic-entity terms. This is not a matter of mere belief, but it is "Known" to be so if you heart-recognize Me and Really "Locate" Me. Heart-Communion with Me is about "Perfect Knowledge" of Me, not mere belief in Me.

If you truly enter into heart-Communion with Me, you "Know" Me in the Non-localized sense—and you are (Thus and Thereby) Un-bound, by Me, from your own localized existence as well.

The appearance of localized existence is going to be destroyed, in time. Every local appearance is going to die. Therefore, it is self-evident that you should make use of the brief occasion of embodiment to Realize That Which Is Non-local—Reality Itself, Prior to time and place and "point of view". Reality Itself Is the Only "God" There <u>Is</u>.

The purpose to which the lifetime should be given is the tacit Realization and the direct Demonstration of Reality Itself. What "causes" the lifetime is all the "machinery" of conditional reality. Nevertheless, that does not mean that the purpose of the lifetime is in the domain of "causes" and "effects". The purpose by which the lifetime should be governed is the Prior and Intrinsic Realization That Transcends conditional existence, Transcends "point of view", Transcends localization, and (therefore) Transcends embodiment (in the localized, egoic sense).

II.

The first six stages of life are all based in "point of view", structured with reference to various modes of the psychophysical structure of the "point-of-view"-based body-mind.

The West is a dimension of the "world" in which people presume things to be a certain way—fundamentally, on the basis of their bondage to the first three stages of life—and they are constantly commanding one another to maintain those presumptions. In the West, everybody is, by socially and culturally patterned tendency, always afraid that people are going to get "too mystical".

In the East, people are becoming more and more "Westernized". Therefore, they are also, more and more, manifesting the "point of view" that you might otherwise find typically in the West. However, if you go deeper into the East, you find people who are associated with the traditional understanding. Because they are acculturated to that understanding, Easterners tend, by socially and culturally patterned tendency, to be rather puritanically intolerant of anything associated with the first three stages of life. Easterners tend to regard anything related to the first three stages of life with suspicion, doubting that what is of a gross material nature can have anything to do with a "pure" Spiritual life.

The characteristic Eastern understanding of life is dictated by the traditional culture of association with the fourth, the fifth, and the sixth stages of life. Even though people in the East, like people in the West, are (generally speaking) initially (from birth and early life) bound up in the first three stages of life, their understanding of the potential of life is culturally governed by the esoteric stages of life and the traditions that have grown out of the fourth, the fifth, and the sixth stages of life.

People in the East should not expect Me to be exclusively Alpha-like in order to satisfy their Eastern expectations. And, similarly, people in the West should not expect Me to be exclusively Omega-like in order to satisfy their Western expectations. I Am <u>Myself</u>—just <u>As</u> I <u>Am</u>. In My Case, there is no "point-of-view"-identity, no localized body-mind-identity, no identity associated with <u>any</u> of the first six stages of life.

I Am exactly as I have Described the seventh stage of life to Be. I <u>Am</u> That Which is to be Realized. Therefore, My Divine Avataric Self-Manifestation is not governed by the characteristics of either the East or the West. My Divine Avataric Self-Manifestation is not "in" the domain of either Alpha or Omega.

III.

There is a cultural divide in the "world", and it is constantly being kept in place by social, cultural, "religious", political, and otherwise "official" means. I am not here to maintain that divide, but to restore the Indivisible Wholeness and the Intrinsic Perfection That is otherwise forgotten in the midst of every "difference".

My Very Person Exceeds both East and West, Exceeds the characteristic limitations of both the Alpha orientation and the Omega orientation.

The current Western preference is to look at everything in terms of brain phenomena—what particular areas of the brain or functional systems of the brain tend to be stimulated by a particular activity (such as, for example, meditation practice), and what outwardly (and even, primarily, socially) observable results tend to occur from such brain-stimulation. Western researchers are always looking for brain changes, physical changes, and social-functioning changes to come about as a result of virtually anything and everything within the domain of human exercise. To investigate phenomena on some other basis is, in the West, essentially taboo.

The many modes of possible meditation practice have originated in a flow of tradition that is not adapted to "Westernized" purposes. Nevertheless, the typical Western approach to investigating meditation reduces and changes it into something it was not originally intended to be. In any case, many traditional meditators (from even all traditions) are now all lined up to go to the laboratories to have the "effectiveness" of their "technique" verified by scientists—but the scientists are only going to measure how meditation affects brain activities, brain functions, and brain centers, and how such brain phenomena affect functional activities and social behaviors in the context of "ordinary" (or gross physical) life.

The great purpose of traditional meditation practice is not merely to produce changes in the functioning of the brain and the behavior of the gross physical and social personality. In fact, if anything, the traditional purpose of meditation is to <u>exceed</u> the brain—the brain as a barrier to the "Knowledge" of Reality (or Truth, or Real God). Thus, traditionally, meditation practice is about going <u>beyond</u> the brain and <u>beyond</u> the gross physical and social personality.

Scientific materialism always wants (and strives) to reduce all human-scale activities (including meditation) to something that is "Godless" (or, certainly, grossly material and non-"metaphysical", in its origin and ongoing status). In other words, scientific materialism specifically excludes anything beyond the brain and the nervous system and the human entity (as it is currently limited and described by conventional science) from the sphere of human purpose or effect or experience.

Scientific materialism is a dogmatic and authoritarian view, and a very negative and suppressive one. This view has made a dreadful mess of the entire "world"-happening. And this view is based entirely on the lie of "point of view", the presumption of separate bodies and separate brains.

The ancients were also (and very elaborately) aware of the mechanisms of the brain and the nervous system. Traditional esotericism is built on such familiarity with the mechanisms of the brain and the nervous system, as well as the subtle dimensions of all aspects of psycho-physical functioning. Nevertheless, the purpose of such esoteric "knowledge" was not merely to become physically healthier, or to improve one's functional mind, or to achieve success as a social personality. Rather, familiarity with the mechanisms of the brain and the nervous system was anciently (and traditionally) used as a means to go beyond limitations, into a greater conditional sphere of "experiential" possibility—and, ultimately, to exceed conditional "experiential" possibility altogether. Thus, the purpose of traditional esoteric practices was to transcend all limitations.

The "scientific materialist establishment" is as dogmatic as the conventional "religious establishment" from which it originally struggled (and has chronically continued to struggle) to differentiate itself. Scientific materialism (in contrast to true science, which is utterly free, or un-prejudiced, enquiry) is, in effect, a dogmatic and authoritarian tradition that limits enquiry rather than allowing and supporting free enquiry. Indeed, scientific materialism plays all kinds of power-games to prevent people from legitimizing kinds of research or views about "reality" that do not "fit" with the philosophy of scientific materialism.

My Divine Avataric Revelation-Word Speaks to everyone, by Means of truly Free Discourse. My Divine Avataric

Revelation-Word must not be "sized down", in an attempt to make It acceptable within the Omega culture of scientific materialism, exoteric "religion", and socio-political "realism", which is now dominating humankind through the systematic application of materialistic (or merely exoteric) philosophy and gross "realism" in every domain of human endeavor. The gross "realism" prejudice is not merely unfortunate—it is "dark". Therefore, My Divine Avataric Work necessarily involves a persistent root-criticism of this gross-minded and "dark" philosophy—and, to counter and replace that "darkness", My Divine Avataric Work is to establish a Unified Whole human, cultural, and social basis for right life in a priorly unified "world". Such Work requires Me to Utter the Reality-Revelation of Perfect Philosophy and to Transcendentally Spiritually Self-Reveal the Perfect Way.

In Reality, the brain is simply a barrier, or a limit—a structure of limitation that functions, essentially, as a locked door. And that door must be unlocked—by Means of the Real Transcendental Spiritual process. Part of what the enterprise of scientific materialism is doing is keeping the brain-door locked tight (and always guarding it), because scientific materialism is based on the absolutization of the notion of "point of view"—and, consequently, the absolutization of the presumption of separateness (and gross "realism").

Scientific materialism (or science based on a materialistic prejudice) tends always to de-sacralize and desecrate its subject of materialistically biased enquiry. The "sacred" and the "holy" are, from the "point of view" of scientific materialism, to be made entirely subject (and subordinate) to grossly prejudiced secular enquiry, without regard for the otherwise "sacred" or "holy" status of the "subject in question". Thus, for example, in the view of scientific materialism, meditation is not about "God", not about super-normal events, not about the transcending of mind, and brain, and body, and gross materiality. In the view of scientific materialism, meditation is merely about the brain. Therefore, in the view of scientific materialism, meditation cannot conceivably be about anything but changing your efficiency of functioning (in brain and body), and, thereby, making you more amenable to social life and gross material productivity.

However, in Reality, the brain is <u>not</u> separate. Reality altogether is Non-separate and Indivisible. Like everything else, brains are participating in Reality Itself—and are, therefore, not separate. The physics of how Non-separation is demonstrated in the context of appearances is a study that is, in the domain of science, still in its infancy—because of the limitations that the "official" dogmas of scientific materialism bring to bear, by disallowing the full spectrum of possibilities from being thought about and examined in a straightforward and un-prejudiced manner. Nevertheless, in due course, it will be discovered—and is, perhaps, beginning to be discovered to some degree—that there are dimensions of the complex of brain and nervous system that originate and always reside in the domain of super-physics, the super-physics of Non-separateness. The super-physics of Non-separateness is the means for finding out that it is not, in fact, true that "when you're dead, you're dead". The super-physics of Non-separateness can also "explain" how, and on what basis, processes of a truly Transcendental Spiritual nature can be entered into—processes that exceed the limitations of the brain and the nervous system and the limitations of the gross physical and apparently separate person.

I Am the Eternal Demonstration of all that is forever Beyond, and of all that must yet become "known". I am not merely a localized consciousness, or a "point-of-view"-consciousness—originating in, and utterly identified with, and reducible to a physical brain, nervous system, and body. Therefore, in My Divine Avataric Self-Manifestation here, I Am the Proof and the Demonstration of the super-physics inherently associated with conditional appearances—and

I Am the Proof and the Demonstration of the all-and-All-Transcending Indivisible Perfect Space That Is Reality Itself. The "Westernized" prejudice that is scientific materialism does not want to allow research into the domain of super-physics—not to mention acknowledging even the possibility of the actuality of that domain to begin with. Scientific materialism does not want to acknowledge anything that exceeds the "dark" (and utterly foolish) philosophy of gross materialism.

Even to use the word "matter" is a throwback to the nineteenth century—as if there have been no scientific advances in physics since then, and as if it still makes sense to talk about "matter" or "materiality" as if "it" were a "something". Truly, "matter" is not a "something" at all. There is only Continuum, only Non-separateness, only Indivisible Reality Itself—only the Single and Self-Evidently Divine "Substance" of Conscious Light Itself.

Like everything else in the conditional domain, brains are not separate. Like everything else in the conditional domain, brains are participants in the Intrinsic Indivisibility of Reality Itself. How that all works can and should be investigated by true and free science. Such investigation, done as free enquiry, is a legitimate human activity—although it is not merely about studying how meditation affects the brain, as such study is currently being done. The "observation" of the super-physics of Non-separateness and the Perfect Realization of the Intrinsic Perfection That Is Reality Itself are not "subjects" that are reducible to mere laboratory testing.

If you want to "find out" about Reality Itself and the Inherent Non-separateness of conditionally apparent phenomena, you must expand your participation beyond the laboratory and the university. You must do the process of "finding out" in the domain of Reality Itself and of the super-physics of Non-separateness Itself. You have to be willing to do so, because such "finding out" is not merely an academic process, nor is it merely a laboratory event.

In My Divine Avataric Teaching-Word, I present clear Arguments as to why the "separatist" view and the view of scientific materialism is not true. My Arguments are a direct (and, hopefully, corrective) Criticism of academic and scientific research as it is now typically done. My Divine Avataric Teaching-Word is an extension of My Person and Realization and Condition. It is My Act of putting into language modes of My Intrinsic Self-Apprehension of Reality Itself.

I am not talking about something that is merely <u>logically</u> so. What I am Revealing is not a matter of theory, and not a matter of ideas. What I am Revealing is Spoken from the "Place" Where "It" <u>Is</u> Always Already Self-Evidently <u>The</u> Case.

My State corresponds to What I otherwise philosophically Propose. I am not proposing a philosophical theory and then "going looking" for it. I am not suggesting, "This Truth is logically the case, so we should look into it some day." I could not even be writing My Revelation-Word if Realization were not Always Already <u>The</u> Case in Me and <u>As</u> Me. Most Perfect Divine Self-Realization Is the Basis on Which I have been Doing <u>all</u> My Divine Avataric Work.

I am not merely speaking philosophy in the academic sense, within the domain of mere ideas. I am Speaking on the Basis of My Own Demonstrated Realization, Which Corresponds to My Inherently egoless State—the Self-State of Reality Itself.

IV.

In terms of the psycho-physics of the human process, the Eastern (or Oriental, or Alpha) orientation wants to open up the "fontanelle" (or the upper reaches of the brain), while the Western (or Occidental, or Omega) orientation wants to lock the "fontanelle" down with a steel plate. Thus, the two orientations are very different—and, indeed, precisely opposite.

The Omega orientation wants to remain fixed in the body, and to go out bodily into the gross "world", as it is apparent to the "self"-presumed gross "point of view". The Alpha orientation wants to withdraw from the body and the "world", and to go "up and out", above the body—even though the Alpha limitation is also rooted in the "self"-presumption of "point of view".

Thus, there are two different orientations of "point of view" common in the "world". The Omega orientation, associated with the first three stages of life, aims to lock down the "fontanelle". The Alpha orientation, associated with the fourth, the fifth, and the sixth stages of life, aims to open up the "fontanelle"—in other words, to exceed the barriers and limits of the brain, but still on the basis of the exercise of "point of view".

Thus, there is the Western (or Occidental, or exoteric) domain of the first three stages of life, and there is the Eastern (or Oriental, or esoteric) domain, of the fourth, the fifth, and the sixth stages of life—but all six developmental stages are founded on the illusion of "point of view". Only the only-by-Me Revealed and Given seventh stage of life Inherently Transcends "point of view".

My Divine Avataric Word challenges both East and West to transcend the principle of "point of view", and the extensions of "point of view"—which are the notions of separateness, relatedness, otherness, and "difference", each played out in the context of a fixed orientation (whether grosser or subtler).

These are the possibilities of "point of view", going in one or the other of two directions. And, on both sides of the "aisle" (so to speak), people speak dogmatically of their own approach as if it were the "Absolute". East and West are either in conflict with one another or running in opposite directions from one another. Such is the egoically "self"-divided sphere of human mummery.

The only-by-Me Revealed and Given Way of Adidam transcends both the Eastern and the Western orientations. The only-by-Me Revealed and Given Way of Adidam is not based on "point of view". Therefore, the only-by-Me Revealed and Given Way of Adidam is not based on identification with either ego-"I" or body-mind—but the only-by-Me Revealed and Given Way of Adidam is based on the Always Prior Self-Apprehension of the Self-Nature, Self-Condition, and Self-State of Reality Itself, and, therefore, the only-by-Me Revealed and Given Way of Adidam proceeds, from the beginning, on the basis of the always prior transcending of ego-"I" and body-mind, or all of "point of view".

V.

The essential limitation of the Great Tradition of humankind—as a whole—is "point of view" (or ego-"I", or separate "self"). Thus, the essential limitation of the Great Tradition of humankind is the presumption of separateness altogether, the presumption that the "world" is divided into "self" and "not-self".

"Point of view" is conditional locatedness. "Point of view" is a location in space-time. In all traditions, East and West, human thinking about Reality is limited by the presumption of space-time-locatedness, or "point of view". The structure of "subject"-and-"object" is the fundamental dichotomy associated with all "point-of-view"-based thinking, or egoic presumptions about Reality.

The characteristic Western (or Occidental, or Omega) strategy is an effort, based on the presumption of space-time-locatedness, to gain control over "objects", or "objectified" reality, or "objectified" space, or "objective" space. When Western (or "Westernized") people refer to "space", they typically mean "out there", or "out in the world", or "outer space". Such is the characteristic sense of Reality from the Western (or Omega) perspective—the perspective of the closed head, or the closed "fontanelle"—which locates "subjective point of view" within the body-mind, and "objective environment" in the grossly apparent sphere.

The characteristic Eastern (or Oriental, or Alpha) strategy, based on the presumption of space-time-locatedness, is an effort to gain control over "subjective" space (or "internal" space, or "inner" space). Therefore, the Eastern (or Alpha) enterprise is an "internalizing" effort—associated with the "method" of dissociative introversion—to explore "point-of-view"-locatedness within.

The West and the East represent a fundamental dichotomy—associated, in both cases, with the presumption of space-time-locatedness, or "point of view".

The dichotomy of "self" and "not-self" is expressed in the differences between East and West, or Alpha and Omega cultures. The Omega (or Western) orientation is associated with exploration and search in the context of the "objectified not-self", or "outer" (or "outside", or "external") space. The Alpha (or Eastern) orientation is associated with exploration and search in the context of the "subjective self", or "inner" (or "inside", or "internal") space.

Both orientations are based on the same principle—of space-time-locatedness, or "point of view". It is simply that the Omega disposition looks in one direction, while the Alpha orientation looks in the other direction. They are looking in opposite directions—but from the same fundamental "point of view". Omega looks to "out" (or "outer" space), while Alpha looks to "in" (or "inner" space).

Omega mind is always looking for the "Cause" of the universe by searching for "it" in "outer" space-time. Therefore, Omega mind is characteristically associated with the notion of a "God" that is the "Creator" of the universe. The universe—or the space-time-located "point of view"—is presumed first.

By contrast, the Alpha traditions, generally speaking, understand the Divine in different terms —as the Source of the "subjective self", or the most interior Condition of the "subjective self".

The West looks for "Outer Cause", while the East looks for "Inner Source". The West looks for the "Cause" of the "not-self", while the East looks for the Source of the "self".

Thus, the Great Tradition, as a totality, is limited to the first six stages of life. The first three stages of life are the exoteric stages of life—which represent the limits of the Omega search. The fourth, the fifth, and the sixth stages of life, or the culture of esotericism, represent the limits of the Alpha search.

Nevertheless, both orientations—Alpha and Omega—are based on the presumption of space-time-located "point of view". Thus, each of the two primary "limbs" of the Great Tradition is looking for "something" in space.

VI.

The seventh stage of life, of which I Am the Divine Avataric Self-Revelation, is the Searchless Way—Prior to "point of view", or space-time-locatedness. The seventh stage of life is the Way of the One and Indivisible Conscious Light—Which Is the Intrinsically "point-of-view"-less Self-Nature, Self-Condition, and Self-State of Reality Itself, and (therefore) of Space Itself.

Space Itself Is the Matrix of the "consideration" of the entire Great Tradition of humankind.

Space Itself Is The Indivisible Matric Of Intrinsically Non-Polarized and Perfectly Conscious Energy (or Conscious Light).

Conscious Light Is the Self-Nature, Self-Condition, and Self-State of Space Itself.

Space Itself Is Conscious Light.

Space Itself Is Reality Itself.

Space Itself Is Divine.

Space Itself Is Perfect Space—and not merely "outer" or "inner" space.

Everything is arising in Perfect Space—Which Is Divine, or Absolute, or Reality Itself.

Modern science—which is, essentially, a Western enterprise in its origins—hypothesizes that the present-time apparent conditional universe arose in a single originating event, generally referred to as the "Big Bang", and that everything that has occurred since the "Big Bang" is (thus) emerging as if from a "point". Furthermore, it is presumed that, before the "Big Bang", there was no space. Thus, the right understanding of "space" (in the cosmic context) is—even from the perspective of modern physics—that, after the "Big Bang", space is the indivisible totality of what is emerging.

The common view is that space is a kind of container, or empty vessel, wherein all kinds of "objects" are appearing. However, the conditionally manifested universe is not merely "in" space. Rather, the conditionally manifested universe is space. Apparent space is the conditional context of all conditional events. Perfect (or Perfectly "point-of-view"-less) Space Is the Source-Nature, the Source-Condition, and the Source-State of the conditionally apparent universe. Reality-Space Is Perfect Space.

What is the Nature, Condition, and State of conditionally apparent space? The Nature, Condition, and State of conditionally apparent space Is Perfect Space (or Indivisible Conscious Light)—One, egoless, Absolute, Prior to space and time, Prior to separateness, Prior to "point of view", Prior to East and West, Prior to Alpha and Omega, Prior to "subject" and "object", Prior to "outside" and "inside", Prior to "self" and "not-self". Perfect Space Is Reality Itself. Perfect Space Is the Perfect Context of all-and-All.

The One and Indivisible and Self-Evidently Divine Conscious Light Is That Which Is both Self-Evident As Perfect Space Itself and Prior to conditionally apparent space. Perfect Space Itself Is Absolute. Time is the context of conditionally apparent space, or the conditionally apparent universe, as perceived or presumed on the basis of "point of view" (or spatial "self"-locatedness). Prior to "point of view" and the space-time-locatedness of the "objectified" universe, There Is Only the Condition That <u>Is</u> Perfect Space Itself—not conditionally apparent space (which is apparent only in the context of time), but That Space Which Is Always Already Prior to time, Always Already Prior to the "Big Bang", Always Already Prior to the conditionally apparent universe.

The notion that the "Big Bang" is associated with a rather local apparition of the universe is not, in any sense, an observation that can be said to (even conditionally) characterize What <u>Is</u>, as a Totality. In the "consideration" of conventional science, there is the possibility of other planes of existence, or other universes—but the observable universe is understood only in the context of space-time. Nevertheless, in every moment, conditionally apparent space is apparent only in the Perfect Context of Perfect Space Itself.

The observable universe can be explored as something "objective", or it can be explored as something "subjective". It can be explored "outside" or "inside". In either case, the exploration is always of the Same Condition—Which <u>Is</u> Perfect Space Itself.

Perfect Space Itself <u>Is</u> Conscious Light. Perfect Space Itself Is also What is, in the esoteric traditions of humankind, called "Spirit", or "Shakti". Conditionally apparent space-time is an apparition of Energy. Perfect Space Itself, the Matrix of all events, may be compared to a fractal, because only Its Own Likenesses are apparent everywhere. At the Root, There Is Conscious Light Itself. Everything emerging in the Perfect Context That Is Perfect Space Itself (or Indivisible Conscious Light) is of Its Nature and in Its Likeness.

Everything emerges in Perfect Space Itself, from Perfect Space Itself, <u>As</u> Perfect Space Itself, <u>As</u> Conscious Light—in other words, As Energy Itself. I refer to Perfect Space Itself as the "Room" of Conscious Light—the "First Room", or the One and Indivisible Self-Nature, Self-Condition, and Self-State of Reality Itself and of all arising appearances. Perfect Space Itself Is the Seed of everything. Everything emerges from Perfect Space Itself—not merely in Perfect Space Itself, but of "It", and As "It". Perfect Space Itself Is the Context of all emergence. Therefore, everything that appears—or can appear—is already in Perfect Space Itself, or Conscious Light Itself. Everything that appears emerges from That "Substance", or That "Substantial" Prior Condition.

Even conditionally apparent space is never (as such) "objectified". When all "objects" are accounted for, there is no "object" remaining that is "space".

It is not possible to separate any "object" from space.

It is not possible to separate the separate "self" from space.

Therefore, space is "self"—and never "not-self".

For this reason, space must be understood to be Always Already Full, and never "Empty" (or an "objectified" and separate "Void", or "Not-Self").

Perfect Space (or Reality-Space) Is the Self-Nature, Self-Condition, and Self-State of the apparently separate "self" and all of "its" presumed "objects".

To Self-Apprehend the space from which one is not separate Is to Self-Apprehend Reality Itself.

The "point of view" (or the space-time-bound separate-"I" presumption) is the "knower" of "objective space" and "subjective space"—or of space as the presumed "empty container" of "outer objects" and "inner objects".

The "Space" That is Self-Evident Perfectly Prior to "point of view" Is the One and Indivisible Conscious Light— the Matrix of all-and-All, and the "Substance" of Which all-and-All that arises conditionally is a merely apparent, non-necessary, and non-binding modification.

The "space" that is either conditionally perceived or, otherwise, mentally evident is a "place"—an "empty container" of apparently separate "external objects" and "internal objects", but without substance of its own.

The "Perfect Space" That Is the Self-Apprehension of Reality Itself Is, Self-Evidently, the Indivisible "Substance" of Which every apparent "object" (whether "external" or "internal") is a non-separate modification (or a mere appearance). The "Substance" of all-and-All is Reality-Space, or the Matrix That Is Perfect Space Itself.

VII.

The searches (or first six stages of life) of humankind are associated with either Alpha or Omega, East or West— exploring either the "objective" side or the "subjective" side of the egoically presumed "subject"-"object" dichotomy. In every subsequent event (East or West), the "subject"-"object" dichotomy (or the presumption of space-time-locatedness, or of "point of view", or of ego-"I") is the root of the pre-selected "limb" of the Great Tradition—Alpha or Omega, esoteric or exoteric.

The only-by-Me Revealed and Given seventh stage of life is the Way That Is Prior to "point of view", Prior to Alpha and Omega—therefore, Prior to all the six searches associated with the Great Tradition of humankind.

The only-by-Me Revealed and Given Way of Adidam is the seventh stage Way—the Way of Reality Itself.

The only-by-Me Revealed and Given Way of Adidam Is the Searchless Way—because the Way of Adidam begins at the Root, or in the context of What Is Prior to "point of view" and appearances and dichotomies and searches.

When the physical eyes are open, you see the infinitely self-multiplied phenomena of conditionally apparent space— the infinite fractalization and fracturing of Perfect Space Itself into space-time-categories, or space-time-"differences". As perception, it all seems vastly complex. Yet, it is also starkly simple—One and Indivisible. What Is At the Root Is Indivisible. What Is Prior Is Indivisible. The Self-Nature, Self-Condition, and Self-State of all-and-All Is Indivisible. It Is Perfect Space Itself, Prior to "point of view". It Is Conscious Light Itself.

Perfect Space Itself Is the Matrix of all conditional events. It is not that there are modes of "cause" and "effect" functioning throughout Perfect Space Itself—as if Perfect Space Itself were a "something", and different from all such events. Perfect Space Itself Is the Very Context and Matrix of all conditionally apparent events, whether they are "outer" or "inner" relative to bodily attention.

Everything is emerging in Perfect Space Itself, of Perfect Space Itself, As Perfect Space Itself, and (Thus) from Perfect Space Itself—as a manifestation of the Potency of Perfect Space Itself (or, in traditional language, the Spirit Itself, or Shakti Itself). Perfect Space Itself Is the "Substance" of Which conditional events are a modification—rather than the "empty place" in Which objects happen and appear in relation to one another.

The esoteric traditions of humankind refer to the "Point of Origin" as the "Beginning", or the "First Cause", or the "Bindu", or the "Single Eye". The "Big Bang" is That Beginning, or First Cause, or Bindu, or Single Eye. Conditionally apparent space-time is an appearance in the Divine Energy, or Spirit, or Shakti—in the "Substantial" Energy That Is Space Itself. However, Prior to the "point" of the "Big Bang", There Is the Indivisibility of the Divine Self-Nature, Self-Condition, and Self-State (or Conscious Light Itself)—Which can be directly Realized by Transcendental Spiritual Means, by Grace of My Divine Avataric Self-Transmission of Conscious Light (and Perfect Space) Itself.

The Self-Transmission of Conscious Light Itself Is What I, since Infancy, have called the "Bright"—Which Is My Own egoless Self-Nature, Self-Condition, and Self-State.

I am not a space-time-located entity—because I <u>Am</u> Conscious Light Itself. I <u>Am</u> Perfect Space Itself—the Very Identity, the Very Matrix, of all appearances and all beings. I am Able to Appear in Association with conditions. And, if I am Invoked, and if there is the right devotional cultivation of the relationship to Me in and via My Incarnate Person, My Inherently egoless and Self-Evidently Divine Self-Nature, Self-Condition, and Self-State is Spontaneously Self-Transmitted.

My Association with This Body-Mind Is the Divine Avataric Event. I Am Self-Transmitted. My Self-Nature, My Self-Condition, My Self-State Is Self-Transmitted.

I do not "cause" Realization in My devotees. Rather, I <u>Am</u> Realization Itself, Self-Evident and Self-Transmitted by the Acausal Transcendental Spiritual Means Inherent in the Perfect Space of My Inherently egoless Self-Nature, Self-Condition, and Self-State.

<u>Such</u> Is the only-by-Me Revealed and Given Way of Adidam. The only-by-Me Revealed and Given Way of Adidam Stands in contrast to the traditions of humankind everywhere, East and West, Alpha and Omega, esoteric and exoteric. <u>All</u> of the first six stages of life have emerged from the psycho-physical conditions of presumed space-time-locatedness, or "point of view", or ego-"I". Only the only-by-Me Revealed and Given seventh stage Way of Adidam Emerges Non-locally and Super-normally In, Of, From, and <u>As</u> the Indivisible Perfect Space and Indivisible Conscious Light of Reality Itself.

Ultimately, East and West, Alpha and Omega, are seeking the Same Reality, the Same Condition—but by looking in opposite directions. The only-by-Me Revealed and Given seventh stage of life Transcends both Alpha and Omega, and the searches associated with each of them. The only-by-Me Revealed and Given seventh stage of life Inherently Transcends the dichotomy of "subject" and "object", and the root-presumption of space-time-locatedness (or ego-"I", or separateness). The only-by-Me Revealed and Given seventh stage of life is not about associative ("objective") extroversion, nor is it about dissociative ("subjective") introversion. The only-by-Me Revealed and Given seventh stage of life is not about any such "method"—Western or Eastern, Omega or Alpha.

In the only-by-Me Revealed and given Way of Adidam, there is no "method" whatsoever. The only-by-Me Revealed and Given Way of Adidam Is the Way of Is. Therefore, the only-by-Me Revealed and Given Way of Adidam is not associated with any of the forms of seeking or any of the "methods" that characterize the first six stages of life, and that (also) inherently characterize the space-time-locatedness of "point of view".

The space-time-locatedness of "point of view" is the intrinsic limitation of Alpha and Omega, East and West. All are suffering and dramatizing the same fault. All of humankind is a mummery based upon this fault. Therefore, the transcending of this fault is the essential requirement for Most Perfect Divine Self-Realization of the egoless, Indivisible, and Self-Evidently Divine Perfect Space and Conscious Light of Reality Itself.

Such Is the only-by-Me Revealed and Given Way of Adidam.

Walk-About To Me

My Self-Submission-Time
Has Come To An End

I.

Beginning in My Infancy, I Demonstrated a Fundamental Impulse to Teach by Means of Self-Submission—with the Intention of Awakening all, through the "Method" of Submitting Myself to the ordinary context of human mind and life. Thus, It was My Intention to Reflect people to themselves, and to Address them relative to their egoic characteristics—not just by Means of verbal Instruction, but also by Living all of this with people and Showing My Revelation-Teaching to them via My Own Bodily Demonstration and Sign.

In Doing all of this, My Intention was to Awaken human beings to Reality Itself, Truth Itself, the Divine Itself—by Means of the right and true devotional relationship to Me. My Intention was to Awaken human beings to rightly and truly devotionally recognize Me—as the basis for practicing "radical" devotion to Me, together with the practice of right life and "Perfect Knowledge" that necessarily accompanies "radical" devotion to Me.

However, My Love-Impulse to Submit—as the Means by Which to Teach and Awaken others—was (over the course of many years) proven to be absolutely fruitless. That Inclination, That Purpose, and That "Method" of My Self-Submission did not—and cannot—work. The only result of My Self-Submission was the "scapegoating" of My Person—while those who came to Me persisted in their bondage and suffering.

The illusions of human beings relative to the virtues supposedly existing in themselves individually and in humankind collectively—illusions that are particularly prevalent in this "late-time", or "dark" epoch—have proven, by Means of My Testing, to be absolute nonsense. All such idealization of humankind and the human individual is patently false. If such idealization had been true, My Effort of Self-Submission would have resulted in the Awakening of human beings.

In My Years of Submission-Work, I Reflected human individuals to themselves and Worked to Awaken them. However, That Submission-to-Reflect was taken to be a sign of Who I Am—rather than being rightly understood as a sign of the Way That I was Teaching. From the beginning of My Divine Avataric Work with My devotees, My Intention was that My Work of Self-Submission would be a temporary "Method"—until Real and True Awakening was evident in My devotees.

It has now been conclusively demonstrated to Me that My "Method" of Self-Submission did not work, and cannot work, and would not ever work. The fact that My "Method" of Self-Submission did not work is a profound matter, with the greatest implications—not only in terms of My Own Divine Avataric Work, but for humankind altogether.

II.

The culture of humankind—as it is—is absolutely false. There are all kinds of modes and levels of falseness about human culture—but, as a totality, human culture is simply false. Human culture is based on an utterly false view of Reality Itself, of the human being, and of the apparent universe.

Therefore, over the many years of My Divine Avataric Self-Submission, the evidence that My Effort of Self-Submission was not going to work (and could not work) steadily grew more and more conclusive. As that conclusion became more and more fully accepted by Me, I began to Work in a different Manner.

A Profound Shift in My Manner of Working occurred on January 11, 1986, with the Initiation of My Divine Avataric Self-"Emergence" Time. Even though I was required to continue My Submission-Work after January 11, 1986, I have, since then, been (fundamentally) simply Revealing My Own Person and Self-State—Which Is the Self-State of Reality

Itself. Thus, in My Speaking and Writing since January 11, 1986, I have simply been Describing the Characteristics of Reality Itself—and, Thus, the Characteristics of My Own Self-State—and the Transcendental Spiritual process that is potential for anyone who rightly and truly approaches Me in the devotional manner.

In the years after January 11, 1986, there was no significant response to Me. Indeed, I was required to endure the demonstration of implacable indifference in human beings, to the point that My Impulse to continue Working in the Manner of Self-Submission utterly Vanished—most conclusively, on July 10, 2007. The fruitlessness of My Effort of Self-Submission became so overwhelmingly obvious that That Effort entirely Fell Away.

Now My "Method" Is <u>Only</u> Self-Revelation. My "Method" is no longer Self-Submission. Divine Avataric Self-Revelation-Only Is the "Method" That has Come About through a Lifetime of Divine Avataric Self-Submission—in the course of Which the fruitlessness of My Self-Submission was conclusively proven.

Direct Self-Revelation of My Own Person and Self-State—Which Is Direct Self-Revelation of the Self-State of Reality Itself—Is the Only Means That Is (and can Be) Effective.

The "Method" of Direct Self-Revelation-<u>Only</u> is <u>not</u> the "Method" Demonstrated by Me during My Years of Self-Submission.

To rightly understand My Divine Avataric Life and Work, it is essential to understand This Change in My Own Approach and My Own Disposition.

III.

The "romantic" (and culturally-transmitted) view of humankind as a "virtuous collective" is particularly evident in the West. That view is the naive presumption that humankind is a mass of "souls" evolving toward some ultimate fulfillment. Thus, the common ("romantic") view refuses to confront the actual nature of the "world"-mummery— persisting in the illusion that human history constitutes a "virtuous progression" that will "move mightily onward".

Through the Demonstration-History of My Own Divine Avataric Life and Work, that "romantic" view of human nature and history has now been <u>conclusively</u> proven to be false. This Testing-Result of My Own Divine Avataric Lifetime Is Profoundly Consequential for human history altogether.

The preciousness of the idealized ego is a lie. Grandiose interpretations of human nature and human history have nothing to do with Truth.

Truth Is Reality Itself. Truth Transcends all "self"- representation on the part of humankind.

Humankind is living in illusion—in an iconic representa- tion of itself. Humankind is "Narcissus", idealizing its own image, and relating to its own mentally-projected image of itself as if that image were an actuality—an actuality that somehow confers a kind of immortality on the ego.

The Only Right and True Way for humankind is the Way of Reality Itself—and not any kind of "way" that idealizes humankind itself.

My Final Work is of an entirely different kind than the Work I have previously Engaged.

My Final Work Is entirely Free of any Inclination to Submit.

My Final Work has nothing whatsoever to do with Submitting to anyone, or to the trends of history.

My Final Work Is <u>Only</u> Myself.

My Final Work Is simply Me here, Revealing Myself.

My Final Work Is simply Direct Divine Self-Revelation— by Avataric Means.

My Final Work Is simply the Self-Revelation of Reality Itself.

My Final Work Is <u>Me</u>—Alone.

IV.

In all the Years of My Divine Avataric Self-Submission-Work, I Related to the gathering of My devotees as if all of My devotees had come to Me for Divine Self-Realization. However, in those Years of Self-Submission, it became (more and more) evident that, in actuality, virtually no one had truly come to Me for Divine Self-Realization. People remained bound in their own "self"-imagery and conventional-mindedness. People remained bound to the messages of the "world"-mummery that congratulate the ego for being itself, and offer it "consumer" fulfillment of itself.

All of that is an illusion—a "dark" joke.

In actuality, humankind is on the march to death—but humankind imagines that it is on the march toward some kind of ultimate "self"-fulfillment. All of that is nothing but propaganda. Nothing of the kind is true. All of that is untrue—not only in terms of the potential destructiveness of this "dark" time, but in terms of the nature of the ego altogether, the ego-disposition to live with its own reflection. Thus, My Work of Self-Submission to humankind—to Reflect humankind back to itself, in its "self"-reflection—necessarily failed. When I "Stirred the pond" while "Narcissus" stared into it, "Narcissus" did not Wake Up. No—"Narcissus" simply took My "Stirring" as a glamorization of "self"-image. I simply became part of the "self"-image with which "Narcissus" was infatuated. In that manner, I was used by people as a means to support egoity. And to the degree that I Made it Obvious that I did not Intend to Offer any such support of egoity, I was punished and ignored by people, and made to wait.

Humankind is a "scapegoat-theatre", enclosing and destroying whatever it touches. During My Years of Self-Submission, I became a part of that suffering, with humankind enclosing Me and controlling Me. Now, I have nothing more to do with that "scapegoat-mummery".

V.

The "scapegoat-method" is the ego's method. Therefore, the "scapegoat-method" accounts for all of human history.

Consequently, the "scapegoat-method" has been the context of My Own Life and Work—until it was proven to My Satisfaction that no right result could be achieved by My Self-Submission to humankind.

Humankind is entirely about the "scapegoat-game". Humankind enacts the "scapegoat-game" in the form of all of its "religions", and all of its traditions (of whatever nature).

Humankind is patterned—culturally and egoically—to enact the mocking and destruction of the Truth-Bearing Force on Earth. Indeed, humankind "scapegoats" everything that comes to its notice—not only in the "religious" or Spiritual context, but in every context. Whatever humankind can enclose in the "middle" of human attention is (thus and thereby) controlled and (ultimately) destroyed.

In Truth, the "Great Tradition" of humankind is the "scapegoating" of the Divine—the control and destruction of That Which Is Divine, the control and destruction of Reality Itself.

Such is the human scale of things.

Such is the ritual of egoity—which has been going on for thousands of years.

Simultaneous with the "scapegoat-mummery", there has always been the Walk-About Way—in which some individuals have responded to Spiritual Masters (in their various first-six-stages-of-life degrees), and in which there is now the possibility of responding to My Unique seventh stage Manifestation here. The Walk-About Way is equally as ancient as the "scapegoat-mummery" (or the "world"-mummery of ego-based humankind).

Thus, there are two fundamental motions enacted by humankind. The common human motion is to persist in the "scapegoat-mummery" (or "world"-mummery). The uncommon human motion is the Walk-About Way, in which some human individuals have participated. The Walk-About Way is a matter of turning to a Spiritual Master on sight, and (thereby) participating in a process of ego-transcending devotion to That Which Is Divine. Throughout human history, both of these motions have been happening.

However, the Walk-About Way has been esoteric, small, not noticed by most. The Walk-About Way has been mythologized by humankind—as if everyone were somehow participating in the Great Matter. It is simply not true that everyone has been participating in the Great Matter. Comparatively speaking, very few (in any generation) have actually turned to a Spiritual Master in any profound and authentic manner. Most have simply "scapegoated" Spiritual Masters—mocked them, shunned them, avoided them.

The Walk-About Way is the primary "method" of Divine Revelation in the world. The Walk-About Way persists regardless of the "signs of the times". And, so, the Walk-About Way must persist now with Me, in My Unique Divine Avataric Incarnation here.

The Perfect Reality-Way is now Given, by Me, to humankind—in the form of the Walk-About opportunity and process in My Divine Avataric Company.

The Perfect Reality-Way I have Revealed and Given is for everyone—not just for the few.

VI.

My Real Divine Avataric Work has only now Begun.
I am no longer Submitting to anyone.
I Am simply Revealing Myself.
I Am here.
The Way of Adidam Is As I have Revealed and Given It. I have Spoken It plainly. My Revelation and Gift of the Way of Adidam now exists in the form of the Literature of My Divine Avataric Word.

My Divine Avataric Word of Instruction is simply Corrective—not Self-Submissive.

Now, I simply Speak the Self-Nature, Self-Condition, and Self-State of Reality Itself—Which Is the Self-Revelation of My Own Person.

Therefore, right approach to Me is not a social approach to Me. Right approach to Me is not coming to Me in order to require Me to talk, or to explain people to themselves. Right approach to Me has nothing to do with any of that.

In every context—including the context of any potential Utterance I may Make—I am simply Revealing Myself.

Now, and forever hereafter, everyone should be moved to Me—in the Walk-About manner.

There is no Walk-About Way if you do not get up and start walking.

If you do not come to Me, you are not practicing the Way of Adidam.

When individuals rightly and truly come to Me, they are fulfilling a profound heart-impulse—regardless of the ego-bondage that may otherwise characterize their lives.

When individuals rightly and truly come to Me, they are moved to Me simply because of My Self-Evidently Divine State—not because I am Submitting to anyone.

People should come into My Company not based on naive "self"-imagery, but (rather) based on a right understanding of Me.

Throughout all the Years of My Self-Submission-Effort, I was "Walking About" to everyone, Submitting Myself to everyone.

Now, My Self-Submission-Time has come to an end—and everybody must start "walking about" to Me.

My Final Work Is <u>Me</u>—Alone

I Am Retired from My Original (or First) Work—of Teaching and Self-Revelation by Means of Extraordinary Submission to would-be devotees and the "world".

My Divine Avataric Word of Teaching and Self-Revelation Is—now, and forever hereafter—Full, Perfect, and Completely Given.

I have Spontaneously Retired into My Own (Always Prior, Native, egoless, Perfect, and Supremely Free) Disposition—without My originally Self-Presumed Teaching Obligations, and without My active First Impulse to Be Self-Revealed by Means of Self-Submission.

In My Supremely Free Disposition, and Perfectly Retired to Me, I constantly bodily Self-Abide at Adi Da Samrajashram, My Always First and Final Hermitage and Blessing-Seat.

I no longer also Wander from My Blessing-Seat—except I am not Fixed in mere "location", and I Am forever now Extended by An Persistent Omni-Presence, all-and-All-Pervading, while I Sit down and here to Lone.

I <u>Am</u> Beyond concerns and attachments and dissociative intentions relative to the body-mind, others, and the "world".

I <u>Am</u> Perfectly Self-Established and Self-Abiding—and, therefore, I <u>Am</u> Beyond the need to seek for My Own Self-Nature, Self-Condition, and Self-State.

I <u>Am</u> Always Already Priorly Self-Established and Self-Abiding—and, therefore, I <u>Am</u> Perfectly Beyond meditation, or any and all need to invert the psycho-physical faculties upon Myself (in order to seek inwardly for My Own egoless Self-Nature, Self-Condition, and Self-State).

I <u>Am</u> the Perfect and Self-Evident "Chosen One" of all My true listening devotees, and of all My true hearing devotees, and of all My true seeing devotees—and of all My devotees who (having listened to Me Perfectly, and having also heard Me Perfectly, and having also seen Me Perfectly) truly practice the "Perfect Practice" of the only-by-Me Revealed and Given Reality-Way of Adidam.

With the Spontaneous Commencement of My Final Retirement from Submission-Work (and, Thus, the Spontaneous Commencement of My Final Work of Divine Avataric Self-"Emergence"), My Avatarically-Born bodily (human) Divine Form Spontaneously Continued, Simply As I Am, in accordance with My Own and egoless Native Disposition (and by virtue of the Inherent Sufficiency of Divine Self-Realization, Itself)—Always Already, Natively, Non-conditionally, and, Thus, Perfectly Self-Established, Beyond and Prior to all motions of mind and body.

I Am Perfectly Beyond limitations.

I Am Perfectly Beyond limited and limiting traditions, methods, and prescriptions—of all kinds.

I Am Perfectly Beyond the search by "self"-indulgence and the search by strategic psycho-physical (and, thus, conditionally dependent and goal-oriented) "self"-negation.

I Am, Natively (Priorly, or Always Already), of the Perfectly egoless State and Disposition—without any conditionally operative "cause" or "reason" Why.

On the Basis of My Own Priorly Perfect Self-State and Native Disposition (and, Thus, by virtue of the Inherent Sufficiency of Divine Self-Realization, Itself), I Am Priorly, Inherently, and Perfectly Self-Established Beyond and Prior to all motions of mind and body.

I Am Divinely Perfectly and Motivelessly Indifferent relative to all psycho-physical and merely conditional possibility.

My active bodily Life-Signs are not purposive "techniques", or strategic "methods" of goal-oriented "practices"— nor are they merely "ideals" to which I seek to conform.

My active bodily Life-Signs are not "purposed" or "achieved" by Me—and, therefore, I have not "achieved" Indifference to body and mind as a result of any seeking, nor do I "maintain" Indifference to body and mind by any "practice" of psycho-physical means.

My active bodily Life-Signs are always a spontaneous characteristic of My Own (Native, egoless, Perfect, and Divine) Self-Nature, Self-Condition, and Self-State.

My active bodily Life-Signs are always a spontaneous characteristic of the Perfectly "world"-Outshining Self-Evidence of My Always Prior and Perfect Transcendental Spiritual Self-Apperception of the egoless Indivisible Conscious Light That <u>Is</u> Reality Itself.

My Own and Perfect Disposition <u>Is</u> Truly Free—and Priorly (and, Thus, Inherently, or Non-conditionally) Free of all identification with the conditionally arising (and merely apparent) body-mind and its conditionally arising (and merely apparent) "world" of function, desire, and seeking.

The natural (apparent) functions of the body (and of the totality of body-mind) are always Perfectly (or Priorly, Inherently, Spontaneously, and egolessly) Self-Managed in Me, and This Disposition (of Perfect Freedom's Prior and Inherent Self-Management of the apparent body-mind) is actively and Motivelessly Demonstrated (and not merely enforced by strategic, or problem-based, or merely idealistic and "self"-suppressive means) within My Free Sannyasin context of (apparent) natural conditions and associations of life.

In practice, Thus and Finally Retired, I am Always Spontaneously (and not strategically) Conserving the (apparent) bodily functions and Spontaneously (and not strategically) Conducting the bodily apparent energies—in Perfect (and Always Prior) Freedom, without submission to the strategically "self"-indulgent (and mentally and bodily degenerative) patterns of egoic and problem-based searches and addictions, and (also) without the strategically "self"-controlling (and mentally and bodily negative) patterns (of egoic and problem-based seeking) that originate from the totality (and the irreducible duality) of the habits that are indigenous to ego-bondage, and without conceding to any merely "prescriptive" rules, or programs, or problem-motivated strategies, or seeking-"methods", or merely conditional (and psycho-physically "self"-applied) "techniques".

Even in <u>all</u> of My Avatarically-Born Lifetime in bodily (human) Divine Form, I have always been Merely (and

Perfectly) Self-Abiding here, Priorly Free, and never bound by any apparent mechanism of conditional identity, or of conditionally apparent action, or of conditionally apparent association.

Whether before or during or beyond My Final Retirement, I <u>Am</u> (<u>As</u> I <u>Am</u>) an Always Already egoless Free and "Radical" (or Divinely Perfectly and egolessly Self-Realized) Renunciate.

In My Finally Retired Divine Indifference, I Am a single and (characteristically, and in My always Prior and persistent Disposition) solitary Sapta Na Sannyasin—always Priorly and Freely without bondage, or content, or egoic "self"-identification relative to natural bodily functions, and, altogether, in every mode of bodily action, Perfectly Self-Managing—and (<u>As Such</u>) I <u>Am</u> (Inherently) Free Merely (and <u>Only</u>) to <u>Be As</u> I <u>Am</u> in My Divine and Avatarically Responsive Transcendental Spiritual Regard of all-and-All.

Relative To the <u>everything</u> that arises, I am neither "for" nor "against"—and, therefore, My Freedom Is a Motiveless Sign, not of "compromise" and "synthesis" between "yes" and "no", but of Intrinsic Non-"difference" and of Divine Indifference.

In My Avatarically-Born bodily (human) Divine Form, I Am Inherently (or Always Already) Free—rather than merely strategically and resultantly (or conditionally) "free".

I Am Divinely Perfectly Free-Born.

I am not Free because of any mental reasoning ("for" or "against"), nor am I Free as a result of any seeking (or any conditionally, or bodily, or psycho-physically, or dualistically motivated and applied strategy, method, or effort).

In My Avatarically-Born bodily (human) Divine Form, I <u>Am</u> Inherently (or Always Already—and, <u>Thus</u>, Perfectly) Free of <u>all</u> the cumulative burdens associated with apparent identity, apparent actions, and apparent associations in the "world".

Because I <u>Am</u> Free, I Am (in My Final Retirement) Beyond the necessity and the concern to Teach.

In My Final Retirement, My Inherent (and <u>Only</u>) Vow and Obligation to all (and All) Is the Intrinsically Silent "Purpose" That <u>Is</u> My egoless, Perfect, Transcendental Spiritual, and Divine Self-Nature, Self-Condition, and Self-State (<u>As</u> "It" <u>Is</u>, and <u>Only</u> In, and Of, and <u>As</u> "Itself").

In My Final Retirement, I Always (Inherently) Recognize whatever (and all) that (apparently) arises to be a transparent (or merely conditionally apparent), non-necessary, and, altogether (and inherently), non-binding modification of My Own (Inherently egoless, and Self-Evidently Divine) Self-Nature, Self-Condition, and Self-State.

I am not merely "meditating upon" Reality Itself (Which <u>Is</u> the Indivisible Divine Truth, Itself)—as if That Which Is to Be egolessly <u>Self</u>-Realized is an "Object" of perception and conception over against an "objectified" separate ego-"self" of Mine.

I <u>Am</u> Prior to "subject" and "object"—or space-time-"location" of "point of view", and "other", and "thing", and "difference".

Rather than "meditate upon" Self-Evidently Divine Reality Itself as "Object" to Me—I Always Already Self-Abide <u>As</u> That, without even the slightest "difference" of "What", and without even the slightest "separateness" of "I".

I <u>Am</u> <u>As</u> Reality Itself <u>Is</u>.

Therefore, I <u>Am</u> Always Already Free <u>As</u> Myself.

I <u>Am</u> (Myself) Free Forever, and here Forever—for the Sake of all-and-All.

Therefore, the only-by-Me Revealed and Given Reality-Way of Adidam for all-and-All Is the devotionally re-oriented life of constantly (to-Me-responsively, and whole bodily) turning to Me, <u>and</u> the "self"-discipline (and inherent equanimity) of right life (through constant to-Me-responsive right obedience to My Word and Person), <u>and</u> the always Priorly ego-transcending life-Realization of "Perfect Knowledge".

As a comprehensive whole, the only-by-Me Revealed and Given Reality-Way of Adidam is the moment to moment practice of whole bodily to-Me-responsive turning toward "self"-disciplined, and "self"-surrendered, and searchless devotional (and, in due course, Transcendental Spiritual) Communion with Me—and, thus and thereby, always whole bodily to-Me-responsively (and tacitly, Prior to all thought) Self-"Locating" Me As My Perfectly egoless State.

At last, the only-by-Me Revealed and Given Reality-Way of Adidam becomes Perfect devotion to Me—by Means of My Transcendental Spiritual Self-Transmission of the "Perfect Practice" of "Radical" (or Always "At-the-Root") Self-Abiding As the egoless Self-Condition That Is not-an-"object".

That Which Is Perfect Is The Conscious Light I Am.

To order
books, tapes, CDs, DVDs, and videos
by and about Adi Da Samraj,
contact the Dawn Horse Press:

1-877-770-0772 (from within North America)

1-707-928-6653 (from outside North America)

Or visit the Dawn Horse Press website:

www.dawnhorsepress.com

ADIDAM

We invite you to find out more about Avatar Adi Da Samraj and the Way of Adidam

■ Find out about our courses, seminars, events, and retreats by calling the regional center nearest you.

AMERICAS
12040 N. Seigler Rd.
Middletown, CA
95461 USA
1-707-928-4936

THE UNITED KINGDOM
uk@adidam.org
0845-330-1008

EUROPE-AFRICA
Annendaalderweg 10
6105 AT Maria Hoop
The Netherlands
31 (0)20 468 1442

PACIFIC-ASIA
12 Seibel Road
Henderson
Auckland 1008
New Zealand
64-9-838-9114

AUSTRALIA
P.O. Box 244
Kew 3101
Victoria
**1800 ADIDAM
(1800-234-326)**

INDIA
F-168 Shree Love-Ananda Marg
Rampath, Shyam Nagar Extn.
Jaipur - 302 019, India
91 (141) 2293080

EMAIL: **correspondence@adidam.org**

■ Order books, tapes, CDs, DVDs, and videos by and about Avatar Adi Da.

1-877-770-0772 (from within North America)
1-707-928-6653 (from outside North America)
order online: **www.dawnhorsepress.com**

■ Visit us online:

www.adidam.org

Explore the online community of Adidam and discover more about Adi Da Samraj and the Way of Adidam.